Mark D. Schuman, Esq.
Carlson Caspers
225 South Sixth Street, Suite 4200
Minneapolis, MN 55402
(612) 436-9600
mschuman@carlsoncaspers.com

This handbook deals with law and procedures in effect at the time of publication, 2012. Questions concerning its content may be directed to the author at the address given above.

TABLE OF CONTENTS

INTRODUCTION

United States patent litigation is complex, lengthy and expensive. Even for large domestic corporations experienced in filing and defending lawsuits, the complexity of United States patent law can make patent litigation confusing. For those unaccustomed to litigation, unfamiliarity with the rules and procedures of the United States judicial system make patent litigation even more daunting.

This guide should give the reader a better perspective on the United States judicial process, particularly as it applies to patent law. After studying this guide, the reader should have a better understanding of the United States court system, its rules and its procedures. This guide should also help the reader have a better understanding of the time and cost involved in United States patent litigation. Armed with this new appreciation of United States patent litigation, a patent litigant will understand better his or her attorney's role in the process. He or she also will understand where expenses are generated and be better able to factor costs into rational business decisions related to the litigation.

THE UNITED STATES COURT SYSTEM

Any discussion of litigation in the United States must begin with a description of how the United States court system is structured.

The United States actually has two separate court systems superimposed on each other. The first court system is the **state court system**. The second court system is the **federal court system**. The state courts have **exclusive jurisdiction** to decide some matters while the federal courts have exclusive jurisdiction to decide others. Sometimes both the state courts and the federal courts have jurisdiction over the same matter. When this occurs, the courts have **concurrent jurisdiction**. When the federal and state courts have concurrent jurisdiction, special rules determine which court will decide the case.

Concurrent jurisdiction rarely applies to United States patent litigation. This is because the federal courts have exclusive jurisdiction over patent infringement disputes and the state courts may not decide them. Any dispute regarding the infringement or validity of a United States patent will be handled in the federal court system.

However, in order to fully understand the federal court system, it is necessary also to understand the state court system.

The State Court System

The United States has fifty states. Each of these states is sovereign and, under the United States Constitution, has its own court system.[1]1 These courts generally handle disputes between residents of that state, control land transactions within the state or handle the prosecution of criminal matters that constitute violations of that state's laws.

Each state has *trial courts*. These are the courts in which witnesses are called and where a decision is rendered by either a judge or a jury. Most states also have an *appellate court* which handles appeals from the trial courts. Some states have an additional level, a *court of final appeal*, which handles appeals from the appellate courts. If a state is not heavily populated, the intermediate appellate court may not exist and an appeal from a trial court is taken directly to the court of final appeal without passing through an intermediate appellate court.

Each state has jurisdiction over who can practice law within that state. Each state also establishes rules regarding how law will be practiced within that state. An attorney usually is registered to practice within his or her state of residence. He or she will be registered to practice law in his or her state of residence after passing a two- or three-day test called a *bar examination*. Occasionally, an attorney will also be registered to practice in a few states other than his or her state of residence. This is usually because the attorney has changed residences while practicing law. It is very unusual to find an attorney who is registered to practice in more than a few states.

---

[1] The United States also has the **District of Columbia** (Washington, D.C.) which, although it is not a state, does have its own court system.

3

An attorney who is registered to practice in a particular state is allowed to practice in that state's courts, including its trial courts, its intermediate appellate court (if that state has one) and its court of final appeal. He or she also may practice in the federal courts located within that state. Registration to practice law in at least one state is a prerequisite to practicing law in the federal court system.

TYPICAL STATE
COURT STRUCTURES

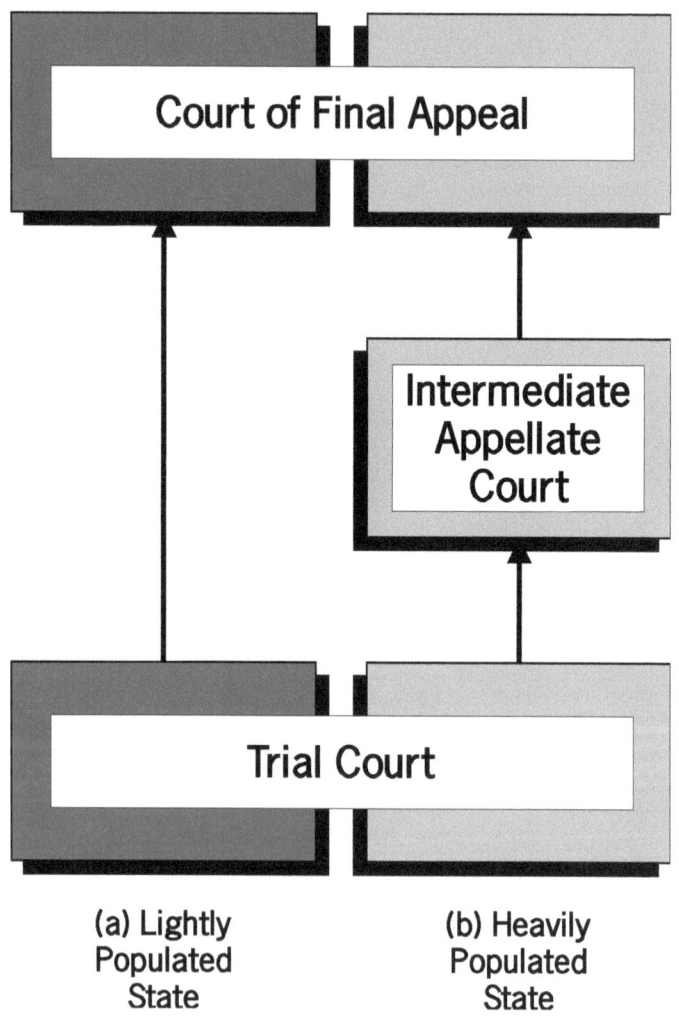

Court of Final Appeal

Intermediate
Appellate
Court

Trial Court

(a) Lightly
Populated
State

(b) Heavily
Populated
State

The Federal Court System

The federal court system is superimposed on the state court system. Each state has at least one *federal district court* within its boundaries. A heavily populated state often will have more than one federal district court within its boundaries. The State of New York, for instance, has four federal district courts: the Eastern, the Western, the Southern and the Northern districts.

A federal district court has jurisdiction within the state in which it is located. If a state has more than one federal district court, then each district court has jurisdiction only over that part of the state defined by its district boundaries.

Appeals from the federal district courts are taken to one of several *federal courts of appeal*. These courts of appeal usually are regional; a number of district courts from adjoining states are grouped together and appeals from them are taken to one appellate court in the region. A group of district courts for purposes of appeal is called a *circuit*. The United States has twelve (12) regional federal circuits. The 8th Circuit Court of Appeals, for instance, has jurisdiction over appeals from the federal district courts located in the states of Minnesota, Iowa, Missouri, Arkansas, North Dakota, South Dakota and Nebraska.

Aside from the regional circuit courts of appeal, there are also special courts of appeal that handle only cases related to specific subjects. One of these, the *Court of Appeals for the Federal Circuit*, handles all of the appeals related to patent law. No matter where a patent lawsuit is tried, its appeal will go to one court, the Court of Appeals for the Federal Circuit

6

BOUNDARIES FOR THE FEDERAL COURTS LOCATED WITHIN THE STATE OF NEW YORK

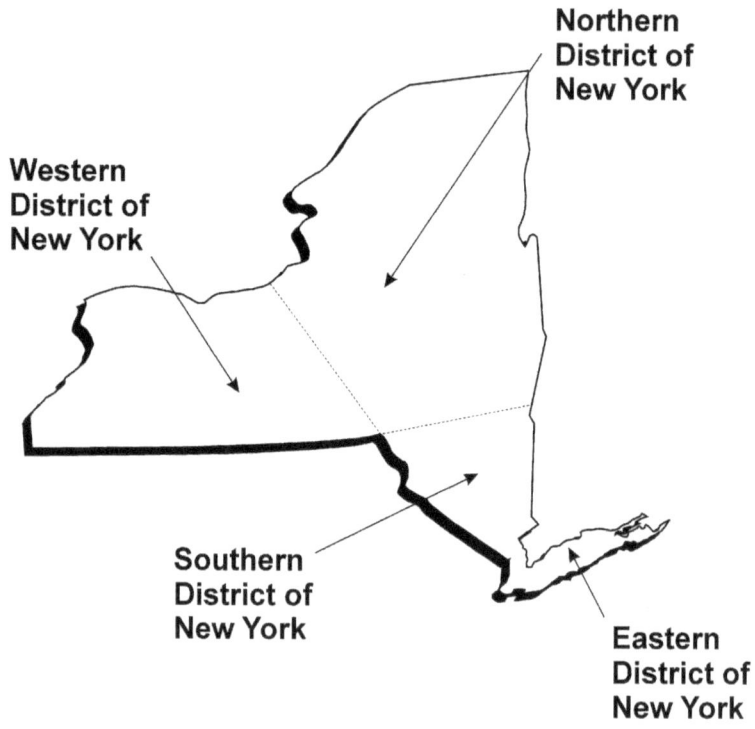

Northern District of New York

Western District of New York

Southern District of New York

Eastern District of New York

BOUNDARIES FOR THE COURTS OF APPEALS FOR THE EIGHTH CICRUIT

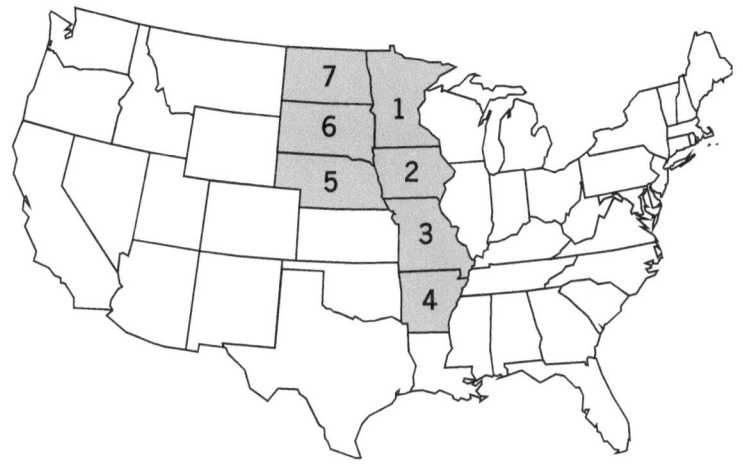

1. Minnesota
2. Iowa
3. Missouri
4. Arkansas
5. Nebraska
6. South Dakota
7. North Dakota

FEDERAL COURT STRUCTURE

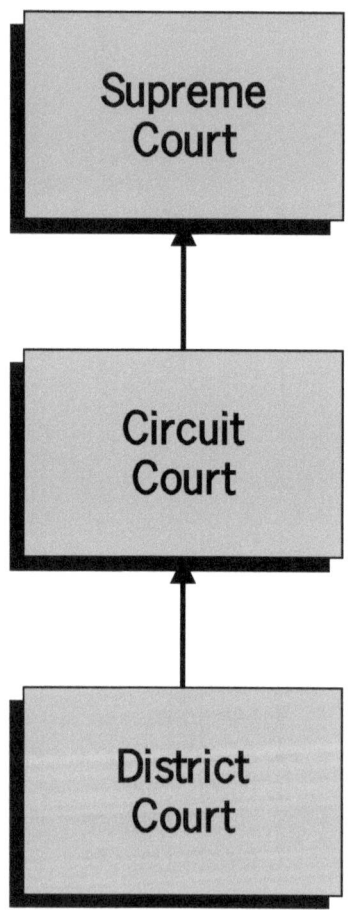

Appeals from decisions of the federal courts of appeal are taken to the **United States Supreme Court**. An appeal to the Supreme Court is discretionary and not a matter of right. If an appeal is lost at the Federal Circuit (or any other federal court of appeal), there is no guarantee that a further appeal will be heard by the Supreme Court. Whether the Supreme Court will hear the appeal is a matter of its own discretion.[2]

Since 1982, only a small number of appeals relating to patents were heard by the Supreme Court, although more cases have been heard in recent years. The chance of having a patent decision reviewed by the Supreme Court is very low.

The Court of Appeals for the Federal Circuit

Whenever a decision is rendered in a federal district court regarding a matter of United States patent law, the decision is appealable to the Court of Appeals for the Federal Circuit, commonly called the *CAFC* or the *Federal Circuit*. The Federal Circuit is located in Washington, D.C.

The Federal Circuit was established in 1982 because the interpretation of the patent laws had become inconsistent between the regional circuit courts of appeal. The United States Congress felt that a uniform interpretation of the patent laws was necessary in order to strengthen the United States patent system. Congress, therefore, created one court to handle all patent appeals. Since the creation of the Federal Circuit in 1982, most of the major conflicts created by the regional circuit courts of appeal regarding the interpretation of the United States patent laws have been eliminated. As a result there is now a more predictable interpretation of the law and, many argue, a strengthened United States patent system.

---

[2] Certain decisions of the federal courts of appeal are appealable to the United States Supreme Court as a matter of right, but they are rare.

Where Attorneys May Practice

Attorneys are registered to practice by the states. Once an attorney is registered to practice in a state, however, he or she also may practice in the federal court system. An attorney who is registered to practice law in the State of Minnesota, therefore, also is allowed to practice in the federal courts located in Minnesota. More importantly, however, he or she also is entitled to practice in the federal courts of any other state.

Federal district courts allow attorneys from outside their state to practice before them. When a district court allows an attorney from outside its state to practice in the state, the court admits that attorney *pro hac vice*. This means that the attorney may practice in that federal district court for the particular pending litigation.

An attorney who is admitted to practice *pro hac vice* in a federal district court is required to retain the services of an attorney within the state to act as an official contact within the state. The attorney chosen from within the district is called *local counsel*.

If an attorney who is licensed to practice in the State of Minnesota wishes to bring a lawsuit in the State of California, he or she will choose local counsel in California, initiate the lawsuit, and ask the district court in California for permission to practice *pro hac vice*. When the district court grants permission to the attorney from Minnesota to practice *pro hac vice*, the attorney can handle the case as though he or she were living in the State of California.

It is important for patent litigants to understand that when they choose an attorney to handle their United States patent litigation, they are not required to choose an attorney located in the state where the lawsuit is pending. They can retain an attorney from any law firm within the United States and that attorney will be able to represent them in the lawsuit. A patent litigant, therefore, should seek to find the best patent attorney in the United States who can handle the case.

11

Judges and Magistrate Judges

The federal district courts, the federal courts of appeal, and the United States Supreme Court all are staffed by *judges* appointed under the Constitution of the United States. Federal judges are appointed for their lifetime. They can be removed from their position only as the result of severe improprieties. Even then, it is difficult to remove them.

Because of their job security, federal judges theoretically are very impartial. Without outside influences affecting their job security, federal judges can decide cases based on what they believe is right, not what will be popular and secure their continued employment.

Most federal judges have the assistance of a *magistrate judge*. Magistrate judges are not appointed for life; they are appointed under a statute and not under the United States Constitution.

Magistrate judges handle the day-to-day affairs of the cases in the federal district courts. Magistrate judges handle discovery matters, routine motions and scheduling. District court judges usually will handle only *dispositive motions* and the actual trial. Dispositive motions are those motions that are important enough that, if decided, they will end the case.

UNITED STATES PATENT LAW

This guide is not meant to be a comprehensive guide to United States patent law. Rather, it is meant to introduce patent litigants to United States patent law and familiarize them with the rules and procedures of the United States court system. Thus, this guide will provide a brief description of the basic concepts of United States patent law.

On September 16, 2011, President Obama signed the Leahy-Smith America Invents Act ("the America Invents Act") into law. This law introduced significant changes to the United States patent system, including switching from a "first to invent" to a "first inventor to file" system for patents applications filed on or after March 16, 2013. The following description applies to applications filed before that date.

Validity

A patent issued from the United States Patent and Trademark Office is presumed valid under the United States patent laws. One way an infringer can seek to defend against a charge of infringement is to assert that the patent is invalid. In order to show invalidity, the infringer must prove that the patent is invalid by **clear and convincing evidence**. This means that the evidence must demonstrate clearly that the patent is invalid. The clear and convincing burden is a difficult one to meet.

Before a patent issues it must meet certain statutory criteria. An accused infringer can seek to invalidate an issued patent by later showing that it failed to meet any of these criteria. They are enumerated below.

Section 101 (Utility)

A patent will be granted only for a new and useful process, machine, manufacture or composition of matter under Section 101 of the United States patent statute. In the past, the *utility* defense was used with some success, but today there is very little that is not considered a new and useful process, machine, manufacture or composition of matter.

Section 102 (Novelty)

An invention must be *novel* under Section 102 of the United States patent statute to be entitled to a valid patent. Section 102 sets out seven instances in which a patent can be invalidated due to novelty reasons. Invalidity defenses based on Section 102 are frequently seen in United States patent litigation.

Section 102 says that a patent is invalid if:

a. the invention was known or used by others in the United States or if it was described in a printed publication (including a patent) anywhere in the world before the invention date of the patent;

b. the invention was described in a printed publication (including a patent) anywhere in the world or on sale in the United States more than one year before the filing date of the patent;

c. the inventor abandoned his or her invention after making it; (Usually, the abandonment must be intentional to invalidate the patent.)

d. a foreign patent was filed more than twelve (12) months before the filing date of the United States patent and the foreign patent issued before the filing date of the United States patent;

14

e. before the invention by a first patent applicant, the same invention was described in a patent application filed by a second patent applicant and the second patent applicant filed his or her application in the United States before the invention date of the first patent applicant;

f. an inventor did not invent the invention found in the patent; (This provision usually applies when an individual *derives* his or her invention from another person and then seeks to patent it as his or her own.)

g. someone has made the invention described in the patent before the applicant's invention date. (This provision also is the basis for United States *interference practice*. Interference practice is outside the scope of this guide. It is sufficient, however, to understand that interference practice seeks to determine who was the first inventor of a patent. United States practice differs from the practice in many countries where only the application date for a patent is relevant in determining who is entitled to ownership of the patent. In the United States, the person who invented the idea first usually is entitled to the patent on it.)

Section 103 (Obviousness)

Even if an invention is novel, under Section 102, the patent still may be invalidated under Section 103 for *obviousness*. If the invention is obvious based on what is already known, the patent is invalid under Section 103.

In novelty determinations, courts look to see if the patented invention was disclosed in a single reference, whether it be a publication, a lab notebook, or another patent. In obviousness determinations, however, two or more references may be combined and looked at at the same time to render an invention obvious.

15

There must be suggestion or motivation, however, to combine the two or more references in order to invalidate an invention as being obvious in view of their combination.

In determining whether an invention is obvious or not, courts generally look at three subjective factors:

1. the level of knowledge and skill of those people working in the area of the invention;

2. the scope of the knowledge of those people working in the area of the invention; and

3. the differences between what was known in the area of invention and the invention.

Due to the inherent difficulty of evaluating these subjective factors, courts also consider objective, **secondary considerations** in obviousness determinations. These include:

1. whether the patentee achieved *commercial success*;

2. whether the patentee solved a *long-felt but unsolved need*;

3. whether others had *failed* before;

4. whether others *copied* patentee's invention; and

5. whether the patentee achieved *unexpected results* with his or her invention.

Section 112

Section 112 of the United States patent statute sets out certain technical requirements that must be met by United States patents. If these requirements are not met, the patent is invalid.

A United States patent must have clear language. It must enable a person who normally works in the area of the invention to make and use the invention without having to perform undue experimentation. In other words, the patent must completely and clearly describe the invention so that it can be utilized by those who work in the area of the invention. If it does not do this, the patent is invalid.

Also, an inventor must disclose the best way of practicing his or her invention in the patent. The inventor's best way is called his *best mode*.

Infringement

A United States patent gives its owner the exclusive right to practice the invention claimed in the patent. When someone, without permission from the patent owner, makes, uses, offers to sell or sells a patented invention within the United States, the patent owner may sue that person for patent infringement. In the United States, a patent owner must prove infringement by a *preponderance of the evidence*. A preponderance of the evidence means that the greater weight of the evidence shows that the patent is infringed.

In determining infringement, a court will first determine whether there is *literal infringement*. There is literal infringement if there is a one-to-one correspondence between the words in a patent claim and the infringing device.

Even if a device does not literally infringe a patent claim, it may still infringe under the doctrine of equivalents. A device can infringe under the *doctrine of equivalents* if it performs substantially the same function in substantially the same way to achieve substantially the same result. If a court finds that a device

17

performs substantially the same function in substantially the same way to achieve substantially the same result as the patent invention, then the device will be found to infringe under the doctrine of equivalents.

The United States patent laws protect both **products** and **processes**. If someone manufactures a product covered by a product patent or utilizes a process covered by a process patent, he will be guilty of direct infringement. Indirect forms of infringement, however, also exist.

One form of indirect infringement is called **contributory infringement**. A party can be guilty of contributory infringement if he supplies a part to a direct infringer and the part has no substantial non-infringing use. The sale of the part to the direct infringer will subject the seller to liability for patent infringement.

Another form of indirect infringement is called **inducement**. Inducement occurs when someone encourages or aids another who directly infringes a patent.

Aside from direct and indirect infringement, a party also may be a patent infringer as a result of activities that occur outside the United States. When an invention is made, used, offered to sell, and sold outside of the United States, the United States patent laws cannot cover the product. If, however, a company generally imports into the United States a patented product or a product which was made by a process patented in the United States, that company will be liable as an infringer. Furthermore, if a company makes *portions* of an infringing product in the United States which will be assembled outside of the United States into a completed infringing product, that company will be liable for infringement even though the actual infringement occurs outside of the United States.

Claim Interpretation

In determining infringement, a court must first interpret the claims of the patent. The claim interpretation process determines exactly what the words in a patent claim mean. By interpreting the claims in a patent, the court decides what the patent covers. The United States Supreme Court decided in a famous case, *Markman v. Westview Instruments,* that claim interpretation is a question of law, to be performed exclusively by the judge, not the jury.

Sometime during the trial or even in the pretrial stage, the court will hold what is known as a **Markman hearing**. A *Markman* hearing is almost like a mini-trial where the parties argue their own versions of the interpretation to be given to the claims. The judge then decides the interpretation that will govern.

In interpreting the claims in a patent, the judge looks at three sources of *intrinsic evidence*:

1.   the claim language;

2.   the main text of the patent; and

3.   the prosecution history (correspondence between patent attorney and the United States Patent and Trademark Office when the patent is still pending).

The court may also consider outside, *extrinsic evidence* when it would be helpful. Extrinsic evidence includes things such as expert testimony, learned treatises, and even sales literature. Courts regularly consider extrinsic evidence as helpful background information for claim interpretation, but must primarily rely on intrinsic evidence.

The *Markman* hearing and claim interpretation are extremely important to the outcome of the case. In many instances, the interpretation given to the claim language is what resolves the question of infringement.

Willful Infringement

A party who has been found liable for infringement of a United States patent must then face judgment on whether that infringement was willful. **Willful infringement** of a patent occurs when someone intentionally disregards the patent rights of another. Willful infringement requires showing that the infringer acted despite an objectively high likelihood that its actions constituted infringement of a valid patent. There is no affirmative obligation to obtain an opinion of counsel.

The penalty for willful infringement is **treble damages**. Treble damages means that a court may multiply the actual damages in the case by three. A party who is guilty of willful infringement also may be ordered to pay the attorney fees of the patent owner.[3] These fees can add up to be a significant cost in patent litigation.

Damages

An infringer must pay **damages** to the patent owner for his or her infringement. Damages usually are determined in one of two ways. An infringer may be liable for actual damages in the form of **lost profits** or he or she may be liable to pay a **reasonable royalty** for the use of the patented invention.

If an accused infringer is found to have willfully infringed a patent or engaged in litigation misconduct, he or she may have to pay treble damages and, possibly, attorney fees.

---

[3] In the United States the prevailing party usually is not entitled to collect attorney fees from the losing party. The patent laws are an exception.

A prevailing party is also entitled to **costs**. Costs include items such as court filing fees and photocopy costs. Costs are usually a minor portion of the damage award. Ironically, it usually costs more money to recover costs than the actual amount of costs that are recovered.

Marking

Before a patentee can collect any damages from an infringer, the infringer has to have been placed on notice that he or she was infringing the patent. Placing the words "patent" or "pat." together with the patent number on a patented product by the patent owner provides the necessary notice to the public that a patent exists on the product and any infringing activity will expose the infringer to damages. If a patented product is not marked, the patentee may not start to collect any damages until he or she notifies the infringer of the infringement and the infringer continues to infringe. The filing of an infringement action constitutes enough notice to the infringer. If there is no product available to mark, there is no way to provide notice of that patent to the public. In that instance, there is no requirement to provide notice to an infringer before damages can be collected.

Lost Profits

A patent owner is entitled to recover the amount of money he or she would have made *but for* the infringement. Courts have interpreted this to mean that a patent owner is entitled to recover his or her **incremental profit** on each product that he or she did not sell because of the infringement.

Incremental profit is the profit that the patent owner would have made if he or she produced just one more patented product. Incremental profit is calculated by subtracting variable expenses from the gross selling price of the patented product. The incremental profit on a product usually is much higher than the actual profit realized on the patented product. Lost profits damages, therefore, may actually exceed the amount of profit actually made by the patent infringer!

Reasonable Royalty

As a minimum, a patent owner is entitled to recover a *reasonable royalty* for the use of his or her invention by the infringer. A reasonable royalty is based on a hypothetical negotiation between a willing patent holder and willing licensee. Because a patent owner may not always be in a profit-making business or may not be able to prove lost profits in part or in total, a reasonable royalty is designed to set a floor on damages.

Courts generally look at the following factors to determine what a reasonable royalty should be:

1. the rates paid by the patent owner and the infringer for the use of other patents comparable to the patent-in-suit;

2. the patent owner's established policy of licensing or not licensing others to use his or her invention;

3. any commercial relationship between the patent owner and the infringer, i.e., whether they are competitors in the same territory or in the same line of business;

4. whether the sale of the patented product promotes the sale of other products that are not patented;

5. the amount of time left until the patent expires;

6. the established profitability of any products made under the patent, the patent's commercial success, and its current popularity;

7. the utility and advantages of the patent over old technology used for obtaining similar purposes;

8. the nature of the patented invention, the character of the commercial product produced by the patent owner and the benefits to those who use the invention;

9. the extent to which the infringer has made use of the patented invention;

10. the portion of the profit or the selling price that is customarily paid for the use of the invention or analogous inventions;

11. the portion of the profit that should be credited to the invention as distinguished from non-patented elements, the manufacturing process, business risks, or significant features or improvements added by the infringer;

12. the opinions and testimony of qualified experts;

13. the amount that a hypothetical licensor and a hypothetical licensee would have agreed upon if both had been reasonably and voluntarily trying to reach an agreement; that is, the amount that a prudent licensee, who desired as a business proposition to obtain a license to manufacture and sell the patented invention, would have been willing to pay as a royalty and yet still be able to make a reasonable profit in doing so.

Reasonable royalty awards in patent cases tend to be much lower than lost profit awards.

Injunctions

In addition to collecting damages for infringement of a patent, a patent owner also may enjoin the infringer from producing future products that infringe. This is called a *permanent injunction*. A court usually will enter a permanent injunction at the end of the trial after the infringer has been found liable for infringement. Occasionally, however, a patent owner will seek to enjoin an infringer at the beginning of a lawsuit. An injunction entered at the beginning of a lawsuit is called a **preliminary injunction**.

A permanent injunction ordinarily will be entered by a court as a matter of course. A preliminary injunction, however, will be entered only in extraordinary circumstances. Extraordinary circumstances can be met by a showing by the patent owner that he or she has a strong likelihood of success against the infringer, that the balance of hardship between the patent owner and the infringer tips in favor of the patent owner, and that the preliminary injunction would not be contrary to the public interest. These are normally difficult to meet unless the patent previously has been litigated and found valid.

If a patent holder is successful in gaining a preliminary injunction, the case usually will settle out of court and will not reach trial. The case usually will settle because a court has decided that the patent owner has a strong likelihood of success even before the case has gone to trial; it is not likely that the court will change its opinion during trial.

Declaratory Judgment Actions

An option that an accused infringer has in patent litigation is to bring a **declaratory judgment** action against the patent owner. A declaratory judgment action is an action brought by the alleged infringer not to collect damages but for a court to make a declaration of invalidity, unenforceability, and noninfringement of the patent. The principal reason for an alleged infringer to bring a declaratory judgment action before being sued by the patentee is to pick where the case will be tried. A declaratory judgment action gives the alleged infringer the advantage of choosing where and when the suit will commence. Where a case is tried can often determine the outcome of a case because of sympathetic juries.

Before a party can bring a declaratory judgment action, however, certain requirements must be met. Because courts will not issue advisory opinions, the alleged infringer can only bring a declaratory judgment action if an actual controversy exists. The United States Constitution empowers the federal courts to only hear cases in which there is an actual controversy. An actual controversy is said to exist in a patent case when there is a substantial controversy between the parties having adverse legal interests, of sufficient immediacy and reality to warrant the issuance of a declaratory judgment. Declaratory judgment jurisdiction generally does not exist merely on the basis that a party learns of the existence of a patent owned by another or perceives such a patent to pose the risk of infringement. Rather, the patentee must make some affirmative act. .

A *cease and desist letter*, a letter from the patentee threatening the infringer with a lawsuit, normally is what the alleged infringer uses to show an apprehension of being sued. However, any communication from the patentee to the infringer that puts the infringer in the position of either pursuing an arguably infringing activity or abandoning that activity may be sufficient to confer declaratory judgment jurisdiction. Therefore, patentees should tread carefully in communicating with potential infringers to avoid triggering declaratory judgment jurisdiction.

FEDERAL COURT LITIGATION

An Overview

The following portion of the guide will detail some of the common procedures followed in the federal district courts, the federal courts of appeal, and the United States Supreme Court. The procedures described below apply to *any* case brought in the federal court system; they are not unique to patent lawsuits. An attempt has been made, however, to discuss how patent lawsuits can be affected by the procedures.

District Court Litigation

Pre-Filing Requirements

Before a plaintiff can file a lawsuit in a federal district court, the plaintiff's attorney must investigate the facts and law to determine that there is a non-frivolous basis for the lawsuit. The Federal Rules of Civil Procedure, Rule 11, specifically states that if an attorney signs a court document, the attorney is certifying that he or she has determined that there is sufficient factual basis for it and that it is supported by the law or a non-frivolous extension of the law.

In a patent case, it is typical to obtain an infringing device and analyze it before filing a suit. One or more claims of the patent are compared with the infringing device and an opinion of infringement is rendered by the attorney. At that point, the suit will be filed.

Occasionally, however, the structure of the accused product cannot be ascertained from an examination of the product, or it is not possible to determine what process was used to manufacture a particular product. There may not be any publicly available information that can be used to determine whether the product or process infringes.

In this situation, an attorney must make a decision whether to proceed with the suit based on the information that is available or to try to obtain the necessary information from the infringer.

As soon as it becomes reasonably clear that litigation is forthcoming, a party should implement a *litigation hold* on all information potentially relevant to the matter to ensure that information is preserved. Employees should be instructed that because litigation is anticipated, they should not destroy any documents or delete any electronic files relating to the facts underlying the litigation (such as an invention, a product, or a patent). Courts can sanction parties for destroying relevant information, so this duty should not be taken lightly.

The Complaint

A lawsuit is commenced by the filing and service of a *complaint*. A complaint is a document which sets out the grievances of the party seeking damages. Usually, it identifies the plaintiff and the defendant and states why the defendant is liable to the plaintiff. A complaint will conclude with a *prayer for relief*, which is a statement of what the plaintiff seeks from the defendant.

The complaint is filed with the clerk of the district court. After it is filed, a copy of the complaint is served on the opposing party or the opposing party's attorney.

The Answer

After the defendant has been served with the complaint, he or she has twenty one (21) days in which to *answer* the complaint. (In certain circumstances, the twenty one (21) day limit is expanded to sixty (60) or ninety (90) days.) In answering the complaint, the defendant either admits or denies the allegations in the complaint. The defendant also may bring his or her own complaint against the plaintiff.

The defendant's complaint may be based on the original complaint or it may be based on any other dispute between the two parties unrelated to the complaint. If a defendant makes a complaint against the plaintiff, it is called a *counterclaim*.

If the defendant files a counterclaim against the plaintiff, the plaintiff then has twenty one (21) days to file his or her answer to the counterclaim. After filing the answer or the answer to the counterclaim (if necessary), the pleadings in the suit are complete. The pleadings frame the issues for the lawsuit and generally can only be modified by an order of the court.

Motions Brought Before the Answer

The Federal Rules of Civil Procedure state that certain motions can be brought in response to a complaint. These are:

1. Lack of jurisdiction over the subject matter;

2. Lack of jurisdiction over the person;

3. Improper venue;

4. Insufficiency of process;

5. Insufficiency of service of process;

6. Failure to state a claim upon which relief can be granted; and

7. Failure to join an indispensable party.

These objections are concerned with whether a defendant is subject to the jurisdiction of the court, whether the court has jurisdiction to hear the particular issues raised by the complaint, whether the location of the lawsuit is appropriate, whether the defendant was properly hailed into court and whether the appropriate parties are present in the lawsuit. Each of these

28

issues should be examined carefully by an attorney prior to filing an answer. Some of these defenses must be raised prior to filing an answer or they are waived and cannot be raised at a later time. Others can be raised at any time.

Discovery

One of the most time-consuming and expensive portions of any lawsuit is the *discovery* period. During discovery, each party has the right to inspect documents of the other party or *third parties* related to the issues in the suit. (Third parties are those parties that are not actually in the lawsuit.) They also have the right to ask written questions of each other regarding contentions and facts related to the suit.

They have the right to take verbal testimony of each other and of third parties in the form of depositions.

All of these procedures are expensive and time-consuming. They also intrude on the regular business activities of both parties. Nonetheless, they are permissible under the Federal Rules of Civil Procedure.

In order to minimize expense, the parties to any lawsuit are expected to meet in good faith early in the lawsuit in order to discuss possible settlement, exchange of discovery information and to formulate a discovery schedule.

The following sections will describe these discovery procedures briefly.

Initial Discovery Disclosures

At the outset of a lawsuit, a party is required to locate and produce to the opposing party information that the disclosing party may use to support its claims or defenses, unless solely for impeachment purposes. These are called the *initial disclosures*. This information will include the names and addresses of individuals that are likely to have discoverable information that the disclosing party may use to support his or her claims or defenses, a copy or a description of all documents and tangible items that the disclosing party may use to support his or her claims or defenses and a computation of damages along with supporting evidence.

After these materials have been gathered, each party is required to turn this information over to their opponent.

Once the pleadings are complete (complaint, answer, etc.), the court will conduct a **scheduling conference** to discuss the case and its schedule with the attorneys. After that conference, the judge will enter a **scheduling order** that sets time limits for the activities in the case.

Parties must, within twenty-one (21) days before the pretrial scheduling conference, confer privately to consider the nature and basis of their claims and defenses. This is called a **Rule 26(f) conference**. Possibilities for a prompt settlement or resolution of the case, arrangements for the initial disclosures, and a proposed discovery plan will be discussed in the Rule 26(f) conference.

The discussions regarding the proposed discovery plan should include subjects on which discovery is needed, the case schedule, the production of **electronically stored information (ESI)**, and any changes that should be made to the limitations on discovery (such as number of depositions and interrogatories), and whether a protective order is necessary.

Attorneys are responsible for arranging the Rule 26(f) conference, for attempting in good faith to agree on the proposed discovery plan, and for submitting to the court within fourteen (14) days of this conference a report outlining the plan.

The parties then have fourteen (14) days after the Rule 26(f) conference to submit the initial disclosures After the Rule 26(f) conference, the parties also can use the other discovery tools to gather information from the other party or from third parties. These discovery tools are:

1. Document requests;

2. Interrogatories;

3. Requests for Admission; and

4. Depositions.

Document Requests

Each party to a suit can request documents relevant to the suit from the other party. Each party in the suit also can request relevant documents from third parties. In either situation, these requests are called *document requests*.

A document request is a list of categories of documents that a party must produce. They are served on the party from whom documents are sought. The party receiving the document requests must agree to produce the requested documents or must object to the production of those documents within thirty (30) days.

A party agreeing to produce documents has the option of

1) producing those documents for inspection as those documents are kept in the ordinary course of business or

2) producing the documents labeled and categorized to correspond to each of the categories in the document request.

Document requests usually are one of the first tools to be used in discovery. After receiving documents, the receiving attorney will review them to determine whether further document requests are necessary. The attorney also will use them as the basis for other forms of discovery.

Electronically Stored Information (ESI)

In responding to document requests, a party must produce not only any paper documents, but also information stored on computers and servers in electronic form, such as emails, spreadsheets, presentations, and Word documents. The process of collecting, reviewing, and producing electronically stored information can be extremely expensive depending on the number and size of the electronic files.

Ordinarily, a party collects files from employees believed to possess relevant information and also conducts broad searches of company files and emails for key words. Those files are then typically loaded into a database and reviewed by attorneys using a review tool on a computer. The reviewing attorneys examine the information for relevance and attorney-client privileged information. After this review is complete, the culled set is then produced to the opposing side, typically in electronic form. Documents that are deemed to be irrelevant or privileged are not produced.

After a party produces its documents, the opposing side then reviews those documents. The documents are typically loaded into a database and reviewed by attorneys using a review tool on a computer. Depending on the volume of documents, the attorneys may conduct key word searches on the database to further limit the number of documents to be reviewed. During the review, the attorneys will code or tag the documents for various issues, such as invalidity or infringement. Those documents will later be used in depositions and at trial.

Interrogatories

The parties may serve written questions on each other after a lawsuit has begun. These written questions are called *interrogatories*. Interrogatories may not be sent to third parties.

Each party is limited to twenty-five (25) interrogatories unless the parties agree to expand the number or the court orders that more interrogatories may be served. In practice, both parties usually agree to serve more interrogatories on each other. In patent cases, for instance, it is not unusual for the parties to serve hundreds of interrogatories on each other.

Interrogatories must be answered or objected to within thirty (30) days of their service. In answering interrogatories, a party may either answer the interrogatory directly or, in certain circumstances, may produce business records in lieu of answering the interrogatory. A party may only produce business records if the answer to the interrogatory may be derived from business records and the burden of abstracting or summarizing the information in the business records is substantially the same for either party.

Requests for Admission

The parties may serve *requests for admission* on each other after the commencement of a suit. Requests for admission may not be served on third parties. Requests for admission ask a party to admit or deny the truth of factual statements. The purpose of requests for admission is to limit the issues that will be decided at trial or to facilitate the introduction of evidence at trial. For example, a party may admit the authenticity of certain documents so that they will not have to be authenticated at trial.

In patent cases, a defendant often asks a plaintiff to admit that it does not infringe some of the claims of the patent. If the plaintiff admits that the defendant does not infringe some of the claims, the issues are substantially narrowed for trial.

If a party refuses to admit a request for admission, and that fact is later proved, the party proving the fact is entitled to recover its costs in proving the fact. In practice this provision is rarely enforced.

Any matter that is admitted in a request for admission is *conclusively established* for purposes of the suit unless the court permits the withdrawal or amendment of the matter admitted. It is extremely important, therefore, to answer all requests for admission carefully.

Requests for admission are a trap for the unwary. Unlike other discovery tools, requests for admission are self-executing. If the requests for admission are not answered within thirty (30) days from the day they are served, the requests are *automatically admitted*! If a party intends to deny requests for admission, he or she must make sure that the denials are made timely.

Depositions

Depositions are the most flexible way of obtaining information in discovery. They are, however, also the most expensive. Depositions usually are held in an informal setting. They might be held in a conference room, in a law office, or in a hotel. The attorneys for each side, the witness and a court reporter will attend the deposition. The attorney requesting the deposition will ask questions of the witness. The opposing attorney will make objections as to the form of the question or if the question seeks information protected by the attorney/client privilege. The witness must answer the questions under oath and have his or her answers recorded by the court reporter.

After the deposition is completed, the court reporter will notify the witness when the record of the testimony is available for review. The witness then may make corrections to the record of the deposition.

Prior to the deposition, the attorney representing the witness (or the witness's employer) will prepare the witness for the deposition by discussing the procedure of the deposition and asking practice questions.

The parties in the suit may take the deposition of each other or of a third party. A person may be deposed in his or her individual capacity or as representative of a corporation. When the deposition is of a representative of a corporation, the party requesting the deposition will ask the corporation to produce a person who will testify regarding specific facts known to the corporation. This is known as a *30(b)(6) deposition*. In a patent case, for instance, a party may ask a corporation to produce a witness who will testify regarding the research and development leading to the patented invention. When asked, a corporation *must* produce a witness who will testify on behalf of the corporation and who will bind the corporation with his or her answers.

When a person's deposition is taken in his or her individual capacity, he or she only will be asked questions about facts within his or her personal knowledge. A deposition of a person in his or her individual capacity cannot bind a corporation.

If a witness is not available to testify at trial, his or her deposition may be read directly into the record. Usually, one person will read the questions and another person will read the answers in open court. The testimony may also be presented by audio or videotape.

A deposition also may be used at trial even if the witness attends the trial. If the witness provides answers that are contrary to the answers he or she provided in the deposition, the attorney can use the deposition to show the inconsistency. Depositions used in this way can be effective tools for establishing that a witness is not credible.

The parties on each side of a lawsuit are entitled to ten (10) depositions unless the court orders otherwise. A deposition consists of a single seven (7) hour deposition day, in most circumstances.

Limitations on Discovery

Discovery in the United States is very liberal. There is not much that cannot be sought and obtained through discovery. There are, however, 3 important limitations on the information that may be obtained through discovery. The first relates to attorney/client privileged communications. The second relates to attorney work product and the third relates to confidential information of a party.

Attorney/Client Privilege

Communications between an attorney and his or her client are *privileged* and not discoverable by the opposing party. In order to qualify for the privilege, the communication must be between only an attorney and a client. No one else can be present during the communication. Furthermore, the communication must be conducted under circumstances of confidentiality. If a communication is conducted in a situation where other people reasonably may hear it or discern its content, the privilege is lost. Last, the communication must center on the giving or receiving of legal advice. General communications with an attorney are not necessarily privileged. Only those communications in which legal advioo is sought or given are privileged.

In some situations, the identity of the client is difficult to ascertain for the purposes of the attorney/client privilege. A determination of who is the "client" can be problematic when a party is a corporation. The safest way to ensure that a privilege exists is to make sure that those people in the corporation who discuss issues with the attorney are part of the corporation's **control group**. A control group of a corporation is that group of people who are actively involved in making decisions on the part of the corporation with respect to the suit. Many corporations have lost their attorney/client privilege through the common practice of sending copies of correspondence between the attorney and the corporation to individuals in the corporation who did not have a need to know the information communicated.

It is best to limit the people who receive correspondence from an attorney. Only those people who need the information for a decision regarding the corporation's actions should receive attorney correspondence.

Attorney Work Product

A party cannot usually receive an attorney's **work product** through discovery. An attorney's work product is all of his or her notes and work that he or she creates in preparing for trial. The reason that an attorney's work product is not discoverable is that it would be unfair for one attorney to reap the benefit of the work of another attorney. Furthermore, it would be unfair to allow one attorney to intrude upon another attorney's preparation of the case. The concept of attorney work product, therefore, is based on a belief that an attorney should be able to prepare his or her case without the other side being able to view his or her strategy.

In certain circumstances, however, a court may order one attorney to turn over his or her work product to another attorney. These circumstances are rare and unusual.

For example, when one attorney has been able to obtain information from witnesses who are no longer available for questioning, a court may order that attorney's observations to be turned over to the other attorney.

Confidential Information

There is no prohibition against the discovery of a company's confidential information. All information, whether confidential or not, is discoverable. The courts, however, have implemented a safeguard against harmful disclosure of confidential information. The safeguard is called a **protective order**

Protective orders generally describe how confidential information will be handled in the lawsuit. In a simple protective order, confidential documents are marked "Confidential" before they are produced to the other party. Thereafter, only attorneys and key personnel for the party will be able to examine the confidential documents. In more complicated protective orders, multiple levels of protection can be established so that very sensitive documents can only be viewed by outside trial counsel, and documents of lesser sensitivity can be viewed on less restrictive terms. The parties usually agree to the form of the protective order and then send it to the court for its approval. The parties generally have great latitude in determining the terms of the protective order so that it fits their needs.

Protective orders carry the full force of a district court's power. A violation of a protective order can result in a **contempt order** by the court. A contempt order may impose sanctions which include fines and imprisonment.

Discovery Motions

A party receiving discovery requests such as interrogatories, requests for admission, or document requests will often object to the requests. If the party asking for the discovery feels that the objections are unwarranted or unjustified, that party may bring a motion to the district court to compel discovery. If the party

38

seeking to compel discovery is successful, the court may award attorney fees to this party bringing the motion.

If a court grants a motion to compel discovery, it will enter an order to that effect. The objecting party must then produce the information. If that party does not produce the information, the court then may impose **sanctions** against it. The sanctions may include:

1. ordering that certain facts in the case will be considered true or false because the information was not produced;

2. ordering that the disobedient party may not oppose certain positions at trial or prohibiting that party from introducing the evidence which was withheld; and

3. ordering that judgment be entered against the disobedient party.

Even though courts have broad powers to compel discovery, they often use them only when other measures have failed. Obtaining discovery from a reluctant party, therefore, can be an expensive and time-consuming process.

Pretrial Preparation and Motions

The parties will begin to prepare for trial after discovery is completed. They will retain experts to testify on their behalf, will make arrangements to have fact witnesses testify on their behalf and will examine the contentions being raised by the other party. They also may take the depositions of their opponent's expert witnesses.

The discovery rules allow the parties to take the depositions of expert witnesses. The rules also require the expert to write and file a report before they are deposed. This is called an **expert report**. Most courts schedule expert depositions at the end of discovery. The depositions of the opposing expert witnesses are extremely important because a party can determine quickly what his or her opponent's position will be at trial.

It is not unusual for one or both of the parties to bring a motion for **summary judgment** after the close of discovery. Summary judgment is a procedure that allows a court to decide the case without going to trial. A party may obtain a summary judgment if there are no significant facts in dispute and that party is entitled to judgment as a matter of law.

The burden for obtaining summary judgment is extremely difficult to meet. Nonetheless, summary judgment motions are common, particularly following a *Markman* hearing. They are common because a successful summary judgment motion will end the case and because the interpretation of a patent claim usually will determine who will win the case. A good trial attorney always will consider whether one or more motions for summary judgment can be brought.

District courts generally order the parties to submit documents called pretrial submissions after the close of discovery. Courts usually require each party to provide a **statement of the case**. A statement of the case describes the nature of the controversy between the parties and describes the evidence and legal contentions that the parties believe support their positions. The statement of the case gives the court a very succinct overview of the case before trial begins.

Courts also require the parties to exchange exhibits prior to trial. After the exhibits are exchanged, each party may object to those exhibits that he or she feels are inappropriate. The objections must be based on the Federal Rules of Evidence. The court usually will rule on the admissibility of the disputed exhibits before trial.

Courts also will consider **motions in limine** during the pretrial period. Motions *in limine* usually seek to exclude evidence that is either irrelevant, inflammatory, or prejudicial. If a party believes that his or her opponent will introduce this type of evidence, he or she may seek to have that evidence excluded before the trial even begins. Another type of motion *in limine* is called a *Daubert* motion. *Daubert* motions seek to exclude an expert's opinions because they are based on unreliable testing methods.

Courts require the parties to submit **jury instructions** if the case will be tried to a jury. Jury instructions are read to the jury at the end of the case and instruct the jury on the law. Each side must submit its own proposed jury instructions. The judge then holds a conference to decide what the jury instructions will be. The court may choose one set of jury instructions over the other or may choose sections from each set of instructions. A party may raise an objection if his or her instructions are not chosen. That objection may form the basis for an appeal if that party loses at trial.

Courts may require the submission of **voir dire** questions if the case will be tried to a jury. *Voir dire* questions are questions that are asked of potential jurors when the jury is being chosen. They help determine whether potential jurors have prejudices that will affect the case. Potential jurors who have prejudices might not be selected to sit on the jury.

After the pretrial submissions are made, the court will hold a **pretrial conference.** In this conference, the judge will decide the issues presented in the pretrial submissions, will rule on the admissibility of exhibits, will set rules for the trial and will generally determine how the case will proceed.

Trial

A judge will set the case for trial at the pretrial conference. A United States law called the Speedy Trial Act gives criminal cases precedence over civil cases, such as patent cases. Therefore, even though a judge sets a trial date, there is a good chance that the case will not be tried on that day. If a criminal trial comes up on that day, it will be tried in preference to the civil case. When a civil case is delayed by a criminal case, the civil case usually is reset for trial months later. Getting to trial can be a very long process in the United States.

Jury Versus Non-Jury Trials

Civil trials in the United States may be handled in one of two ways. They may be tried to a jury or they may be tried to a judge. When they are tried to a judge they are called **bench trials**.

Civil cases are tried as bench trials unless one of the parties requests a jury trial. Then, under the United States Constitution, the case must be tried to a jury.

There are procedural differences between jury and bench trials. In jury trials, judges are more inclined to control how the evidence is introduced. This is because jurors are not skilled in the rules of evidence. Judges, therefore, must filter the evidence so that only the proper evidence is presented to the jury. In bench trials, however, judges usually are more lenient in allowing evidence to be introduced. This is because judges are skilled in the rules of evidence, and will properly discard evidence mentally which is not appropriate.

In jury trials, unlike bench trials, jurors will be instructed on the law by way of jury instructions. The jury instructions are read after the case has been completed and before the jury begins its deliberations. The jury instructions are very detailed and can take an hour or more to read. Jury instructions are not used when the case is a bench trial. The judge is presumed to know the law.

There are different motions that can be made during a jury trial as opposed to a bench trial. After the close of all the evidence in a jury trial, either party may bring a motion for a **judgment as a matter of law** or **JMOL**. The standard for granting a judgment as a matter of law is the same standard that is used for granting summary judgment. The party requesting a judgment as a matter of law must show that the evidence is so clear that no reasonable jury could rule in any other way.

A motion for a judgment as a matter of law usually is denied by the court. It is denied because if a reasonable jury could not rule in any other way, then the jury should rule correctly. If the jury somehow rules contrary to how a reasonable jury would rule, the motion for judgment as a matter of law can be renewed at that time.

A renewed motion for judgment as a matter of law is the last safeguard against a jury which has decided a case absolutely contrary to the law or the evidence. It also safeguards against jury verdicts based on emotion or prejudice. A renewed motion for judgment as a matter of law will be granted only if the decision reached by the jury is a decision that no reasonable jury could have reached after viewing all the evidence. Judgments as a matter of law are rarely granted.

Aside from the differences listed above, jury and bench trials follow the same procedures. These will be outlined below.

Opening Statements

The first part of a trial is the presentation of **opening statements**. The opening statements allow each attorney to put the case in context and to provide an overall framework for the evidence that will be presented during the trial. The evidence at trial will come from each witness's personal knowledge. As a result, the evidence usually is not presented in a story-like fashion and can be confusing.

The opening statements allow the attorneys to provide the judge or jury with an overview of what the evidence will show. Then, when the judge or jury hears the evidence they will know how the evidence fits into the case.

The plaintiff makes his or her opening statement first. The defendant then may follow with his or her opening statement or may wait to present his or her opening statement until after the plaintiff has presented all of his or her evidence. Defendants usually present their opening statements immediately after the plaintiff presents his or her opening statement.

Presentation of Evidence

The parties present their evidence after opening statements. The plaintiff presents his or her evidence first. The plaintiff will call his or her witnesses. Each witness will sit on the witness stand and will give an oath to provide truthful testimony under penalty of perjury. Factual witnesses will testify regarding facts in their knowledge and expert witnesses will testify regarding their opinions.

In patent cases it is common to have an expert who will testify on the technology, an expert who will testify with respect to damages and an expert who will testify with respect to patent law.

The party who calls a witness will conduct the first examination of the witness. This examination is called *direct examination*. Direct examination of a witness involves eliciting testimony from the witness through the use of *open-ended questions*. Open-ended questions are questions such as: who, how, what, when, where and why. Except in extraordinary circumstances, a person conducting direct examination cannot ask *leading questions*. Leading questions are those questions which allow only for a "yes" or a "no" answer.

When the attorney has completed his or her direct examination of the witness, he or she will state that he or she has no further questions for the witness. The opposing attorney then has the chance to *cross-examine* the witness. The rules for cross-examination are much different than those for direct examination. An attorney on cross-examination is allowed to use leading questions. Leading questions provide much more control over the witness' answers and therefore focus the answers to those specific areas which the cross-examining attorney wishes to cover. Furthermore, leading questions do not provide room for the witness to avoid answering particularly sensitive questions.

Leading questions are an important trial tool. Through cross-examination, an opposing party seeks to show that the witness is not trustworthy, does not remember the facts, is exaggerating the facts, or does not even have any personal knowledge of the facts that were a part of his or her earlier testimony.

An attorney may only cross-examine a witness with respect to those areas that were brought out during direct examination. A skillful questioner, therefore, on direct examination, may purposely omit certain areas of testimony if the testimony in those areas might be damaging during cross-examination.

When the attorney has completed his or her cross-examination of the witness, the attorney will state that he has no further questions. The direct examiner then will have an opportunity to conduct *redirect examination*. Redirect examination is like direct examination but is limited to only those areas which were covered in cross-examination. Redirect examination is used to clarify points raised during cross-examination. The attorney must again use open-ended questions during redirect examination.

The testimony of a witness is complete after redirect examination and the witness will be dismissed from the witness stand.

The court will admit *trial exhibits* into evidence during trial. Trial exhibits provide facts or demonstrate expert testimony. Trial exhibits must be marked by the court reporter who is recording the trial testimony. After the exhibit is marked, the exhibit is shown to opposing counsel. If there is no objection from opposing counsel, the witness will be asked to identify the exhibit and to describe what it is and what it says. If there is sufficient reason to allow the exhibit into evidence, the judge then will rule the exhibit into evidence. If the exhibit is not ruled into evidence, it may not be used in deciding the case.

An attorney may ask the court to take *judicial notice* of certain facts during trial. If a court takes judicial notice of a fact, the fact is established without proof. A court may take judicial notice of any fact that is readily ascertainable from common sources. The use of judicial notice shortens the trial because the parties do not have to prove matters that are a matter of common knowledge or public record.

Closing Arguments

After all the evidence in the case has been presented, the attorneys give their *closing arguments*. Unlike opening statements, closing arguments are not limited to a factual presentation of the evidence. Rather, they may argue how the case should be decided. In presenting their closing arguments, the attorneys may not refer to any facts that were not ruled into evidence or which were excluded from evidence during the trial. The attorneys may, however, use any of the facts which are in evidence to argue that the case should be decided one way or the other.

The plaintiff presents his or her closing argument first. The defendant concludes the trial with his or her closing argument.

A decision will be rendered after the closing arguments. If the case is a bench trial, the judge will take the case under advisement and issue a written decision later. The written opinion might take months.

If the case is a jury trial, the court will read the jury instructions to the jury after the closing arguments. After the jury instructions have been read, the court will dismiss the jury to a closed room where they will deliberate on the facts of the case and reach a decision. When they have reached a decision, the jury will return to the courtroom and announce their decision. Unlike a bench trial, the decision in a jury trial is rendered within hours or days of closing arguments.

Post-trial Motions

The losing party has ten (10) days in which to seek post-trial relief from the court. The two major forms of post-trial relief are a **motion for a new trial** and a renewed judgment as a matter of law.

A motion for a new trial will be granted if the court feels that there were severe mistakes made during the trial which were so prejudicial to one party that, in fairness, the case should be retried.

A court may grant a renewed judgment as a matter of law if the court finds that no reasonable jury could have decided the case the way it did. Absent extreme prejudice, a judgment as a matter of law is unlikely to be granted.

Alternative Dispute Resolution (ADR)

Courts and patent litigants increasingly are seeking ways to resolve their disputes outside of court. These various procedures are generically called **Alternative Dispute Resolution** or **ADR**. Litigants are using ADR to avoid the time and money typically associated with full trials. Courts are using ADR to clear their busy trial schedules.

Two common ways for litigants to resolve their disputes *outside* of court are through **mediation** and **arbitration**. There are specific rules that govern each of these proceedings. The rules are governed:

1. by standardized rules written and approved by certain organizations. One organization that has promulgated rules for mediation and arbitration is the **World Intellectual Property Law Association (WIPO)**; or

2. by rules to which both of the parties have agreed.

Another ADR procedure is to use **Early Neutral Evaluation** or **ENE**. An ENE uses a neutral expert in the field to examine both parties' positions and to attempt to give each side an educated evaluation of their case.

Courts often use another technique to help the parties resolve their differences. A common practice is for a court to schedule a **mini trial**. A mini trial is an abbreviated trial which is presented to the judge or other decision maker. Typically, witness testimony is limited or totally eliminated. Rather, each attorney presents their view of the evidence and argues their client's position. At the conclusion of the mini trial, an advisory opinion is rendered. The advisory opinion gives the parties a non-biased preview of how a full trial may turn out. Often, after a mini trial, the parties decide to settle the lawsuit rather than risk a trial.

A patent litigant in the United States probably will be exposed to some form of ADR as the trend toward their use increases.

International Trade Commission (ITC)

Another option for patentees seeking to quickly enforce patents is by filing a complaint with the International Trade Commission (ITC). In the patent context, ITC proceedings are only available for products imported into the United States. However, ITC actions are typically resolved much faster than a patent infringement case in federal court. By law, the case must be concluded in 18 months.

ITC actions are initiated by filing a complaint. Within 30 days of the filing of the complaint, the ITC determines whether it will conduct an investigation. If the ITC decides to proceed with an investigation, it refers the investigation to an **Administrative Law Judge** (ALJ) and assigns an investigative attorney who represents the public interest in the investigation. The ITC also identifies the entities that may participate in the investigation.

The investigation is conducted similarly to infringement actions brought in federal court. A formal evidentiary hearing similar to a trial in federal court is held. Following the hearing, the ALJ issues an Initial Determination. The ITC may then review and adopt, modify or reverse the Initial Determination.

If the ITC determines that the accused products infringe a patent, money damages are not available. Rather, the ITC may issue an Exclusion Order barring the products at issue from entry into the United States. Additionally, the ITC may issue a Cease and Desist Order directing a party to cease certain activities. These orders are enforced by the United States Customs and Border Protection. Appeals of the orders are heard by the Court of Appeals for the Federal Circuit (CAFC).

An ITC action and a Federal infringement case are independent proceedings. They may be brought and run concurrently. Often, however, when they are brought together, a court may stay its action pending a decision from the ITC to avoid duplication.

Appellate Court Litigation

The losing party may appeal an adverse decision in the case to one of the federal courts of appeal.

Appeals from patent cases go to one court, The Court of Appeals for the Federal Circuit (CAFC). A notice of appeal must be filed within thirty (30) days after the case has been decided. If a party fails to file a timely notice of appeal, he or she will irrevocably lose the opportunity to appeal the case.

The notice of appeal is filed with the district court that decided the case. The district court then assembles the record and sends it to the court of appeals. Upon receipt of the record, the court of appeals dockets the appeal and sends a notice of docketing to each party.

The appealing party, called the *appellant*, must file his or her brief within sixty (60) days after receiving the notice of docketing. The appellant's brief will explain why the decision is in error and should be reversed. Not all errors that occur during a trial are errors that will cause a reversal of the case. Only errors that are prejudicial will cause a reversal. A district court is allowed to make mistakes during the case as long as those mistakes do not substantially prejudice the rights of the parties.

The errors that are typically alleged by an appellant fall into three categories. They are:

1. factual errors;

2. legal errors; and

3. abuses of discretion by the district court.

A *factual error* occurs when a district court concludes that something is a fact when there is no evidence to support that conclusion. The party alleging a factual error must show that the factual conclusion of the district court was *clearly erroneous*. A factual conclusion is clearly erroneous when there is no evidence from which a reasonable person could find that the fact was indeed true. If two plausible versions of a fact are presented at trial, it is not clearly erroneous for the judge or jury to decide that one version is correct and the other is not correct.

A *legal error* occurs when the judge deciding the case misinterprets the law or reads the wrong law to the jury in the jury instructions. In order to show legal error, the party only must show what the correct law is and why the judge's view of the law was incorrect.

Many decisions that a judge makes at trial are not covered by specific rules. When they are not covered by specific rules, the decision is left to the discretion of the judge. A judge abuses his or her discretion when a decision is so far outside the bounds of normal conduct that it is wholly unreasonable. It is very difficult to show an *abuse of discretion.*

The party opposing the appeal, called the *appellee*, must file his or her opposing brief within forty (40) days after the appellant files his or her brief. The opposing brief can only argue those matters argued in the appellant's brief. The opposing brief must show that there was no legal error committed by the district court, that the factual determinations of the district court were not clearly erroneous, and that the district court did not abuse its discretion.

Fourteen (14) days after the appellee files his or her opposing brief, the appellant files his or her response. The response may only argue those items raised by the appellee's opposing brief.

The briefing on appeal is complete after the appellant files a response. Shortly thereafter the case will be set for hearing.

The hearings at the federal courts of appeal are called *oral arguments*. The appellant presents his or her oral arguments first. The court, usually comprising three judges, may question the attorney regarding his or her positions. Questioning by the court during oral arguments is common in patent appeals.

The appellant has thirty (30) minutes <u>total</u> for his or her oral argument. The appellant, if he or she requests, may reserve some time out of the thirty (30) minutes for **rebuttal**. Rebuttal is argument that is made after the appellee's oral argument. An appellant will normally exercise this option to reserve time for rebuttal.

The appellee presents his or her arguments second. Like the appellant, the appellee has thirty (30) minutes for his or her argument. Unlike the appellant, however, the appellee has no opportunity for rebuttal and therefore will use the entire thirty (30) minutes at once.

After the appellee's oral argument, the appellant will have the chance to rebut with his or her remaining time. Rebuttal arguments are limited strictly to issues that were raised by the appellee in his or her oral argument.

At the conclusion of oral arguments, the case will be taken under advisement by the court. Some months later, a written decision will be rendered.

Supreme Court Litigation

An appeal to the federal circuit courts of appeal can be taken as a matter of right, but an appeal to the United States Supreme Court cannot be taken as a matter of right. The Supreme Court has sole discretion on which cases it will hear and which ones it will not. The vast majority of parties who ask the Supreme Court to hear their cases never have those cases heard by the Supreme Court.

The request which asks the Supreme Court to hear a case is called a **writ of certiorari**. Statistics show that the chance of the Supreme Court actually hearing a patent case is very low.

Assuming a *writ of certiorari* is granted, however, a Supreme Court appeal is much the same as an appeal to a circuit court of appeals. Because Supreme Court review of any particular case is rare, there will be no further discussion of Supreme Court procedures in this guide.

COSTS AND TIME TABLES

Patent litigation is very complex and, therefore, consumes large amounts of time. Patent litigation also is very expensive.

It is difficult to estimate how long it takes to start a lawsuit and to have it decided. It is not unusual, however, for discovery in a patent case to last between one and two years. In addition to that, it may take an additional six to eight months to have the case tried. If the case is a jury trial, the decision will be returned right away. If the case is a bench trial, a written decision may take many months or even up to a year.

An appeal to the Federal Circuit normally takes about eight months to one year.

If the Supreme Court decides to hear the case, a decision generally will be rendered within one year. This is because the Supreme Court sits in sessions that last one year. The Supreme Court decides all the cases that it hears in a session before that session is concluded, except in unusual circumstances.

Costs in patent litigation vary depending upon the complexity of the case. They will also vary depending upon how expensive the attorneys are. Attorneys on the East and West coasts can be more expensive than attorneys in the Midwest. The **American Intellectual Property Law Association** (**AIPLA**) surveys its members to determine the cost of patent litigation around the United States. The survey reports the costs of patent litigation by city. In 2011, the survey showed that the mean cost of patent litigation by Washington, D.C. firms through trial was $7,609,000 for cases involving more than $25,000,000 of risk. The same case tried by a New York firm was $7,691,000. The same case tried by a Minneapolis firm was $5,713,000. The figures given above were estimated from cases in which the average value at risk was greater than $25 million (the difference between best possible and worst possible outcome was $25 million). These figures can only serve as estimates and are intended to show the *relative* cost differences between counsel in the Midwest and the East coast attorneys. The actual time and costs involved will vary with each case and how much money is at stake.

Surveys are not available for the cost of appealing a district court's decision to the Federal Circuit. Typically, however, an appeal will cost between $100,000 and $200,000. In a complex case it may cost more.

Appeals to the Supreme Court are rare and, therefore, each case dictates its own budget. Generally, however, the cost of taking an appeal to the Supreme Court will exceed the cost of taking an appeal to the Federal Circuit.

TRENDS IN PATENT CASES

There are very strong trends that have occurred within patent litigation over the last 40 years. Although the trend over the last 40 years has been for the number of patent cases filed in district courts to increase, the percentage of cases that complete a trial has been decreasing.

In 1970, 4.3 percent of all cases filed were resolved after a jury trial. By 2001, that percentage had dropped to 1.5 percent. Similarly, in 1970, 10 percent of all cases filed were resolved after either a bench or jury trial. By 2001, that percentage had dropped to 2.2 percent. It is clear that only a very small percentage of the cases that are filed now actually go through trial. Current, reliable statistics are not available.

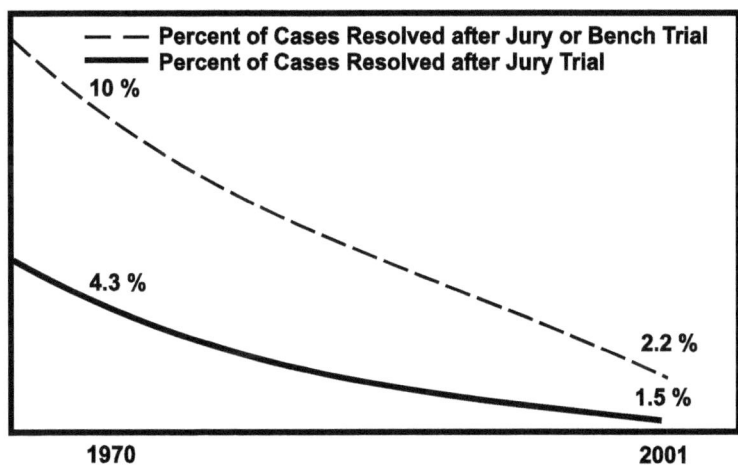

Statistics also show that many more cases are being decided on summary judgment before they have a chance to go to trial. For patent cases, statistics show that in 2001, the total number of appeals was 403. Of those 403 appeals, only 83 were from a bench or jury trial. The remaining appeals were mostly summary judgment rulings. Current, reliable statistics are not available.

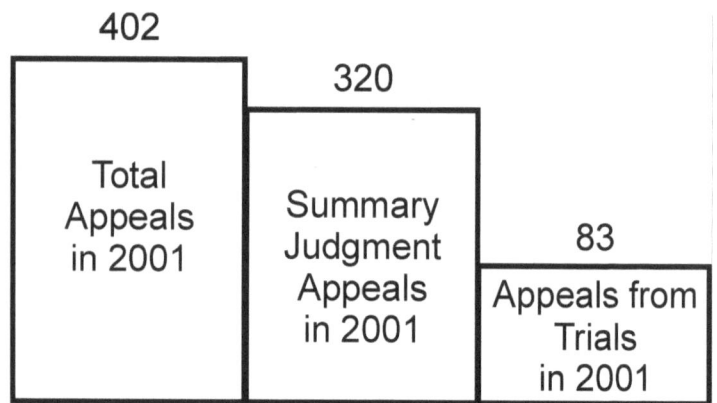

It is the authors' opinion that the statistics are a direct result of the impact of the *Markman* case and the resulting *Markman* hearings in which courts determine claim interpretation before trial. Once the claim interpretation is completed, summary judgment is almost always appropriate because the alleged infringing structure is usually not a matter of factual dispute. Thus, if the claim is interpreted in favor of the plaintiff, the plaintiff will win on summary judgment and if the claim is interpreted in favor of the defendant, the defendant will win on summary judgment.

Knowing these statistics, a patent litigant should choose its attorney in patent litigation to maximize the chance of obtaining a favorable outcome.

It is the authors' opinion that because the great majority of patent cases are decided on summary judgment after a *Markman* hearing, a patent litigant should seek out a litigator who is technically trained rather than a litigator who is not technically trained. It does not seem wise to engage a patent litigator merely for his or her trial skills--either to the bench or to a jury--when only

2 percent of the cases ever go to trial in front of a jury or to the bench. Cases are being won or lost at the *Markman* hearing and a patent litigant should find counsel who can critically examine the technology and expose the weaknesses of the opponent's case from both a technical and legal standpoint. A patent litigant should engage counsel who can win a *Markman* hearing, not a trial.

CONCLUSION

This manual has provided the reader with some background in United States patent law and the United States judicial system. With this background, the reader should be equipped with the basic principles of patent litigation in the United States. This manual should give the reader a better understanding of United States patent litigation and more tools to effectively make business decisions regarding it.

ABOUT THE AUTHORS:

Mark D. Schuman

mschuman@carlsoncaspers.com
612-436-9650

Mark is a named partner with the firm.

Mark's practice encompasses contested matters in the United States District Courts, state courts and administrative agencies. Mark has participated in numerous district court trials to both the bench and jury on matters related to patents, trademarks and other intellectual property rights. He also has participated in numerous *Markman* hearings. Mark obtained a temporary restraining order and seizure order against a Taiwanese company. He also has headed ANDA litigation over the drugs Prilosec®, Protonix®, Zantac® oral solution, Axert®, and Nitro-Dur®.

Mark's technology exposure has been broad. He has headed litigation involving electronic circuitry, mechanical devices, optics, surface roughness, chemical compositions, adhesives, software and pharmaceutical drugs.

Mark's other work experiences include advising clients on licensing, and providing infringement and validity opinions. He has advised clients on design-around strategies.

Mark is active in bar organizations and is the past Chair of AIPLA's Patent Litigation Committee. He also served on AIPLA's nomination committee.

Education
University of Wisconsin-Madison
J.D., *cum laude*
Order of the Coif
Editor, *Law Review*
Northwestern University
B.S. Chemical Engineering, with distinction
Tau Beta Pi
Omega Chi Epsilon

Bar Admissions
Minnesota Supreme Court
Wisconsin Supreme Court
U.S. District Court for the District of Minnesota
U.S. District Court for the Eastern District of Michigan
U.S. District Court for the Eastern District of Wisconsin
U.S. District Court for the Federal Circuit
U.S. Court of Appeals for the Eighth Federal Circuit
U.S. Court of Appeals for the Tenth Federal Circuit
U.S. Patent and Trademark Office
United States Supreme Court

Sarah M. Stensland

sstensland@carlsoncaspers.com
612-436-9651

Sarah practices intellectual property law with a focus on patent litigation, using her background in chemical engineering to effectively understand her clients' technologies. Sarah is a volunteer attorney with the Children's Law Center and is an active member of the Federal Bar Association. In law school, Sarah was a staff member of the *William Mitchell Law Review*. Prior to law school, Sarah worked in the quality department of General Mills, testing various products and raw materials. During her years as a student at the University of Iowa, Sarah worked in a genetic research lab, assisting in experiments to understand the function and regulation of particular ion channels that are linked to hypertension and cystic fibrosis. In 2012, *Super Lawyers* named Sarah a "Rising Star".

Education
University of Iowa
B.S., Chemical Engineering
William Mitchell College of Law
J.D., *magna cum laude*
William Mitchell Law Review, Vol. 31, Staff Member

Bar Admissions
Minnesota Supreme Court
U.S. District Court for the District of Minnesota
U.S. Court of Appeals for the Federal Circuit

INDEX

64

www.ingramcontent.com/pod-product-compliance
Lightning Source LLC
Chambersburg PA
CBHW040811200526
45159CB00022B/239